DIRECT RESPONSE RADIO

*The Way to Greater Profit with Measurable
Radio Advertising*

What Matters,

BY: BRETT J. ASTOR AND JEFFREY R. SMALL

ISBN: 1-4196-8222-9
ISBN-13: 978-1419682223

Visit www.booksurge.com to order additional copies.

TABLE OF CONTENTS

Acknowledgements

Before we began putting words to paper, we were told that writing a book is almost never easy. Moreover, for first-time authors it can be overwhelming. We can now confirm that it is indeed a challenging undertaking. This book would not have been completed were it not for the timely support, encouragement and efforts of many people along the way.

We would like to thank our colleagues James Clark and Jason Cormier for first planting the "write a book" seed years ago. They have remained supportive and are two of the brightest people we've had the pleasure of working with.

Many thanks to our editor, Gail Cato, who has steered us clear of a few confusing expressions and otherwise provided us with numerous valuable suggestions for enhancing the clarity of this book. A special thank you to Robert Leonard and Christina Iannucci for their extra-duty efforts as reviewers. Your feedback helped confirm and distill many of our ideas.

Last but not least, we want to express our heartfelt gratitude to the entire team at Strategic Media, Inc., with whom we've traveled the path of relentless testing and unending analysis to uncover *what works* and *what matters* in direct response radio advertising. The insights distilled from the intelligent work of many people comprise the basis of this book. A very special thanks to the core team at SMI: Rhonda, Heidi, Joe, Matt, Jennifer, Bob, Pam, Ronnie, Christina, Kara, and Sarah.

Introduction

Why did we write this book? And why do you want to read it?

Search for books on radio advertising and you'll find two types. One type is the academic volume that goes deep into the nuts and bolts of theory and media formulas, *none of which was developed by people required to deliver a profit for their customers.* The other type, written by radio salespeople, hits you hard with subjective and biased puffery about why you should advertise on radio. Neither of these is useful to someone who wants to *understand* radio advertising and receive guidance about the actions that produce the best, most profitable business results.

Radio advertising is intriguing because it is so underrated, so overlooked. TV and print advertising are infinitely sexier than radio. They're visible, and they're tangible. However, on important dimensions of cost, targetability, and reach, radio outperforms the marquee mediums of TV and print. More recently, online advertising has gained traction and larger portions of advertising budgets, yet it functions more as a demand capture medium and doesn't match radio when it comes to demand generation.

Yet in spite of the momentum against it, radio advertising delivers the goods as perhaps the most efficient medium that quickly and inexpensively reaches 94% of the US population over twelve years old. In fact, three of the top ten radio advertisers in 2005 were TV networks—ABC, CBS, and Fox (according to Media Monitors, LLC). Yes, radio advertising works so well that even TV networks use it to boost TV audience size.

So the story about radio advertising is one of how the emotional desire for tangible, sexier advertising overwhelms the rational need for achieving business objectives. It's a classic case of crossed wires. And that spells opportunity for the businesspeople who can uncross them and see radio for what it is (and, of course, isn't).

However, if the uncrossing of wires were the whole story, we wouldn't have written this book. It turns out that many have tried radio advertising and decided, "It doesn't work for us." The nexus of this book came last year at a direct response industry event where we heard the same story a number of times within a short period. The basic theme was, "We tried radio advertising and it didn't work for us."

If you heard this once, you'd just say, "Well, OK, radio can't work for *everybody*." But after the third person said the same thing, we started to ask more questions about these situations where radio "didn't work." We found out that the radio tests—if you can call them tests—these people conducted were doomed to fail because they followed few, if any, of the fundamentals of what we've learned works in direct response radio. In all three cases, and most others we've heard since, these intelligent, successful businesses turned to their current general agency to "test" radio. It turns out all general agencies say yes when you ask if they "do radio," even though they don't have an expertise in radio. Why? Because they don't want to lose the client to another agency. So the agency approaches radio advertising the same way it does TV, print, and online because that's all the agency knows. Now think about what happens when radio fails (because it will, if you approach it the same way as TV or print or online). The general agency can point to that failed test and say, "TV is where you need to be," and radio advertising is never again considered. How convenient. Convenient, that is, for the general agency that would rather do more glamorous and *much* more profitable (for the agency) TV work.

Creating a profitable radio advertising campaign isn't easy. The way to success is not obvious. Unlike TV, which provides both visual and auditory information, and print, which provides static visual information, radio is one dimensional and fleeting. As a result, radio requires a different, perhaps broader and more nuanced, skill set than TV or print or even online advertising. Radio is often called the "theater of the mind," and advertising successfully on the radio requires a solid understanding of how the human mind processes auditory information—information that is often delivered in the midst of other stimuli.

If you speak to radio advertising industry sales representatives about advertising with them, you'll get spiffy sales pitches and some fancy graphs and charts with impressive rankings. They'll make it sound easy. We find it unfortunate that the radio industry—the owners of radio stations and radio networks—has chosen this shortsighted approach that takes the money but leaves the needs of radio advertisers (their paying customers) completely unmet. A victim of an outdated, sales-driven mentality, the radio industry is focused solely on increasing listenership numbers, looking shortsightedly toward each season's new Arbitron numbers much the way public companies manage their stock prices by dancing with Wall Street's quarterly expectations. Nowhere does the radio industry provide information about what actually *works* in radio advertising. Not guesswork, not opinion, not theory, and not the CEO of major radio holding companies advocating in national newspapers[1] that radio ads should sound like entertainment so listeners won't change the station. The radio industry behaves like a sales machine, screaming, "Your customers listen to our station!" as though we should not only take the industry's word for it, but also believe that audience size is all that matters. The radio industry is not focused on helping paying customers apply what works and what doesn't so those customers can get the most value from radio advertising. No, we've been left to figure that out on our own.

The purpose of this book is very straightforward:

To provide businesspeople with a practical, straightforward guide to understanding direct response radio advertising, and how to use it to profitably grow a business.

If you're looking for a deep dive into theories and history, you won't find it here. We are writing for the busy marketing manager, CEO or vice president who wants to get a practical understanding of radio advertising and how to go about using it as a tool for profitable business growth.

About Us

Who are we to write this book? Jeff started working in radio advertising in 1995 when the direct response radio advertising industry was first taking off. He gained experience both as a direct response radio media buyer, working in a direct marketing company, as well as on the sales side, working with radio stations. Brett has held senior marketing and management roles in small, medium, and Fortune 50 direct marketing companies for nearly twelve years. At the time of this writing, we've worked together for almost eight years as the owners of Strategic Media, Inc., a leading direct response radio advertising agency. The vision that led to Strategic Media began with a deep curiosity—what would happen if we combined the best of radio advertising techniques with the sophisticated database-enabled practices of traditional direct marketers that use catalogs and direct mail? To satisfy our curiosity, we built a direct response radio agency *not* on demo reels, fancy lunches, and flashy dog-and-pony showmanship, but rather on something very straightforward and likely much more boring: substance. Our sole focus is creating radio advertising campaigns that generate measurable results and profitable new customers. The foundation of this focus is our radio advertising results database, which contains the results of over a thousand radio advertising tests relating to hundreds of radio advertising variables. We know of no other such database that captures what works in radio advertising, nor one that does as much to help businesses capture the potential that radio advertising offers their businesses.

CHAPTER 1

Direct Response Radio Advertising 101

> It has taken more than a hundred scientists two years to find
> out how to make the product in question; I have been given thirty
> days to create its personality and plan its launching. If I do my
> job well, I shall contribute as much as the hundred scientists to
> the success of this product.
>
> —David Ogilvy, *Confessions of an Advertising Man*

Direct response radio advertising, at its core, fulfills the same business need regardless of what type of business you are in. That business need is customer acquisition.

Whether you own a direct-to-consumer model business, a retail business, a Web business, or some combination thereof, you need to acquire new customers if you want to grow. Even if you don't want to grow, you need to acquire new customers to replace the ones you're losing through ordinary attrition.

Throw out all you think you know about advertising, radio advertising, and direct response advertising. It's best to begin with a big, clean whiteboard. Once your mind is clear, we want you to think about the following concepts as the backdrop for the rest of the book.

1. What is Direct Response?

The first concept one must understand is that of "direct response." We can understand direct response in two ways.

First we can define it: Direct response advertising is *a form of advertising that is designed to elicit a response that can be measured in such a way as to provide a concrete and swift evaluation of its effectiveness.* Direct response advertising is measurable and accountable for generating data that will demonstrate its effectiveness.

The other way to understand direct response advertising is to contrast it with other approaches to advertising. In the direct response world, we often refer to "brand" advertising as a form of advertising designed primarily to influence memory recall of a product, service, or "brand," and often to associate that product or service with some positive emotion. Brand advertising is not designed to be related directly to sales on any kind of granular level. Rather, it is typically held accountable for producing results in terms of "awareness," "recall" (aided or unaided), and sometimes "intent to buy."

In direct response radio, your ad contains a call to action with a specific tracking mechanism. Often, this tracking mechanism is a "call now" prompt with a toll-free phone number or a unique Web URL. With direct response, you track the results of your ad in terms of calls, orders, customers, leads, sales, revenue, and profits that result from the airing of those ads. Then you compare the revenue you received to the cost to air that ad and you determine whether the effort resulted in profit (revenue − costs = profit). You do more of what "works" (profit) and no more of what doesn't work (no profit).

To be clear, we are not saying that one way (brand or direct response) is better than another. Each has its own merits, and shortcomings. Further, direct response advertising does not advocate *against,* nor abdicate any responsibility for, building a brand. Rather, direct response campaigns are designed to build a brand in a measurable, accountable way. Evidence abounds that direct response radio builds admired brands. GEICO is a brand that has been built through direct response radio advertising. As is Proactiv Solutions. And Quicken Home Loans. The list goes on.

2. A Highway from Your Business to Your Potential Customers

Think of radio advertising as a 5,000-lane highway from your business to groups—station audiences—of your potential customers. The many lanes on this highway are the many different radio stations and radio networks that are available for you to air your radio advertisement on. You send your message to your potential customers on these "lanes."

The lanes are clustered in such a way that they reach groups—collections of customers—with similar tastes and demographic profiles. Therefore, some of these lanes lead to groups that have a high concentration of people who match your target customer profile. These are the lanes you want to develop a strategy for dominating and protecting from competitive intrusion, as they can provide you a stream of new profits.

Holding costs equal, advertising on lanes with a high concentration of your potential customers is more profitable than advertising on lanes with a lower concentration of your target customer profile. The groupings of lanes are the radio formats, which are used in radio advertising to enhance the efficiency of, or return on, advertising dollars.

3. Radio Advertising Is a Profit Driver, Not a Cost Center

One thing many businesspeople we talk to can't seem to put out of their minds is the question, "How much does it cost to advertise on radio?" The problem with this question is that embedded in it is the presupposition that radio advertising is a cost. The concept that one needs to fully grasp is that radio advertising is not a cost center. That is, it does not stand alone without any relation to revenue or profit. It is detrimental to think of direct response radio advertising as a cost because that leads to managing it as though it's a cost, which means minimizing or eliminating it with the intention to increase profit. Decreasing spending on direct response radio will decrease profits because direct response radio advertising—by its very definition—is a profit driver. If it's not driving a profit, it would not exist—or, at the very least, it would not be called direct response radio advertising, but instead "brand" or "awareness" advertising. Profitability is an inherent characteristic of direct response radio advertising.

The more beneficial way to think about direct response radio is as an investment. With that perspective, you will think about, and focus on, maximizing the return you receive on it.

CHAPTER 2

Will Direct Response Radio Work for You?

The aim of advertising is not to state the facts about a
product, but to sell a solution or a dream.

—Philip Kotler, *Professor of marketing and
author of Marketing Management*

That's probably the first answer you want from this book.
"Is my product or service the kind that 'works' in radio advertising?" "How do I know I'll make a profit with radio?"

One look at the following list of businesses, products,
events, and services categories that have found success with
direct response radio advertising shows that the list of what
works in radio advertising is long—much longer than what
doesn't work.

Financial Services (loans, insurance—think GEICO among others—debt consolidation offerings, different brokerage product offerings, and the like),

Intellectual Property or informational products (wealth building, parenting, fitness, anxiety/stress reduction, weight loss, and similar types of products),

Nutritional Supplements (solution-specific products targeted at any of the various top health concerns),

Beauty (skin, hair, teeth, weight),

Fitness (promotions for various home fitness products and routines),

Seminars (promoting an upcoming seminar in specific markets),

Hard goods (computers, GPS, other new or specialized products),

Retail, driving foot traffic to support general or specific promotions at local retail stores as well as Web retail sales. P&G uses radio to support in-store promotions of its products. Retailer Home Depot is one of the biggest radio advertisers, as is the category of automobile sales. McDonald's is usually among the top ten radio advertisers. Web sites like Priceline.com, eHarmony.com, and Overstock.com have all used radio advertising extensively to build their companies.

Other business categories include auction Web sites, discount buying sites, music, computer repair, employment opportunities, business opportunities, and local professional practices like dental, eye (especially high-margin services like LASIK surgery), chiropractic, acupuncture, and massage.

Table: Top Ten Radio Advertisers in 2006[ii]

2005	2006	Account	Parent
1	1	Geico	Berkshire Hathaway
2	2	McDonald's	McDonald's Corp.
3	3	Verizon Wireless	Verizon Communications
4	4	Home Depot	Home Depot, Inc.
7	5	Fox TV Network	Fox Broadcasting
9	6	Shane Co.	Shane Co.
10	7	AutoZone	AutoZone, Inc.
16	8	Lowe's	Lowe's Companies
46	9	Proactiv Solution	Guthy-Renker Corp.
12	10	Kohl's	Kohl's Corp.

Source: Media Monitors, LLC.

Note that the number one radio advertiser in this table for two years running is Geico, a direct response radio advertiser.

As long and varied as this list already is, what is incredible is that it is still growing. Every year many enterprising businesspeople figure out a new way to leverage radio advertising to help a different business category grow.

What doesn't work in radio advertising? This nearly always boils down to *how* radio advertising is used, not the specific product or service itself. For example, we would not recommend using direct response radio for selling perishable packaged goods such as cereal or cheese. However, direct response advertising can be very effective in support of a product introduction, a special promotion at local stores, and to drive trial. Another example of using radio advertising in a way that doesn't work is characterizing your product or service as preventative, or otherwise solving a problem that someone doesn't yet have. We talk more about this all too common mistake later in the book.

Misunderstanding Radio

The biggest misconception that we hear about radio advertising is the one that goes something like, "If a product has to be demonstrated before anyone will be interested, it won't work on radio." Yet this has been disproved many times. Let's take the classic direct response category of skin care.

There was a time in the direct response world when everyone thought that skin care products could be successfully advertised only with DRTV or DR print because potential customers just *had* to see the before-and-after results. But that assumption has been proven to be completely incorrect as many skin care companies have turned to radio and made—literally—hundreds of millions of dollars (in profit, not just revenue) resulting from direct response radio advertising. As one prominent example, you'll note in the table above that Proactiv Solution, a skin care product, was the ninth most advertised product on radio in 2006.

These skin care marketers have proved the one fundamental axiom of direct response radio advertising: When the radio creative is done expertly, it is possible to do two key things that are required for success in direct response radio: 1) create a vivid picture in people's minds that captures attention, and 2) convey information that entices the potential customer to take an action. *Then the business must have a plan for turning that potential customer into a long-term customer.* When a campaign reportedly fails in radio, it's usually not a failing of radio per se, rather a failing of the *application of radio advertising* to the business or campaign in question.

The truth is this: there is only one way to find out whether direct response radio will work for you. And that way is to test.

First, make sure you have something unique to offer the world—that means a unique product, product characteristic, offer, or otherwise. "Me-too" essentially means copycat, undifferentiated. You can be different or innovative in many different aspects of your offering, but if your product is a me-too offering or if your ad presents your product or service in a me-too way, you'll get poor results.

Second, have a plan to maximize lifetime value of the customers you'll acquire. The focus can be on the first sale, with upsells and conversions from free or risk-free enticements. Or the focus can be on cultivating additional transactions with each new customer. The best approach is a combination of the two.

Third, test. It's worth reiterating because, as we've demonstrated above, the list of what works in radio advertising isn't set in stone; it's long and growing. You can't know for sure whether (or how) you'll be successful until you test.

CHAPTER 3

Four Reasons Radio Advertising Is So Powerful

By painting word pictures about these products (or services), the advertiser allows the listener to fantasize about them. Radio's power—both as a selling and as an entertainment medium—is generated by the listener's imagination. [Radio] offers the direct marketer an unbeatable combination: the immediacy of broadcast and the selective audience of print.

—Alvin Eicoff, *Or Your Money Back*

1. Radio Reaches Nearly Everyone

An advertising medium must reach your target customers or it provides no benefit. Radio has a wide-scale appeal to consumers. Even with the alternatives available today, listening patterns appear to be stable, indicating that radio remains a popular consumer choice. The nearly 14,000 radio stations (approximately 8,800 FM, 5,000 AM) broadcasting across the United States together reach over 94% of the US population over twelve years old each week, according to Arbitron's American Radio Listening Trends report. With radio, there is rarely a question of whether you'll be able to reach your target customer.

2. Radio Reaches Those People Efficiently

How do you advertise efficiently? Through targeting—by paying to reach an audience of people with a high concentration of your desired customer. Radio can do that very well because radio stations are grouped into "formats."

The Value of Radio Formats

Radio formats are usually thought of as delineations based on the type of programming—the type of music or the host (on-air personality) the station puts on the air. That's true, but what's more relevant to advertisers is that each format aggregates a distinctive group of people. As a result, radio formats make targeting with radio advertising both possible and effective. Targeting is the act of directing your message to the right people. Therefore, targeting is the key to how an advertising medium efficiently reaches a target customer. This is important because higher efficiency essentially means you're not paying to reach people who a) you don't want as customers, or b) don't care about your offering anyway. Radio owes a large part of its advertising power to its ability to target efficiently, which is derived by its segmentation by format.

As a result, dollars spent on radio advertising are more efficient, generating a greater return on investment. With the right data, for example, your radio advertising agency can tailor your media plan so your message reaches moms between the ages of 34 and 45. Here is a summary of the formats that reach corresponding demographics[iii] (note that further targeting is possible by sex and other variables beyond age):

Age Target	Format(s)
Teens 12-17	Primarily CHR*, some Urban, Alternative
Adults 18-24	CHR, more Alternative, Urban preference
Adults 25-34	Alternative, Rock, CHR, some Urban, AC
Adults 35-44	Rock, AC* primarily
Adults 45-54	Oldies, AC
Adults 55-64	Classical, New AC
Adults 65+	Adult Standards, Classical, News Talk

*CHR is Contemporary Hit Radio. AC is Adult Contemporary.

Age information is only the beginning of the targetability of radio. For any given format, we can know much more about audience listening habits. Let's look at two different formats, alternative and country, and look at what we know about who we'll reach by advertising on these formats.[iv]

Characteristics of people who listen to the **Alternative Rock format.**

- 63% male, 37% female
- Over 83% are less than forty-four years old
- Adults twenty-five to thirty-four account for almost 28% of the audience
- Listening location: 38% car, 31% home, 28% work
- Geographic skew toward New England, Mountain, and Pacific regions
- 18% more likely to have children in the home (49% of listeners)
- 36.5% earn more than $75k/year
- More likely than any other format to use online banking
- #1 format in movie attendance
- High fast-food restaurant usage (31% have eaten at a fast-food restaurant five or more times within last thirty days)

As illuminating as it is just to see what can be known about a particular format's audience, it is not until you compare the similarities and differences of two formats that you begin to appreciate the full power of radio advertising that stems from the structure of radio into formats.

Characteristics of people who listen to the **Country** format:

- 46.8% male, 53.2% female
- 49% are over forty-five years old
- Adults twenty-five to forty-four comprise 35.1% of listeners while adults fifty-five and over are nearly 30% of listeners
- Listening location: 26.2% work, 37.6% car, 33.5% home
- Geographic skew: primarily, the center of the US and the Southeast; secondarily, the Western Mountains and Great Lakes regions
- 14.8% are college graduates, 37.8% are high school graduates
- 21.5% earn > $75k/yr., 18.9% earn < $25k/yr.
- 62.3% married, 46.5% with at least one child
- 76.8% own their home
- 34.4% Republican, 26.6% Democrat
- Heavy Wal-Mart shoppers—92% shop at Wal-Mart, Target, or both

3. Radio Reaches Those People for a Low Cost

On both creative development and media costs, radio advertising beats TV advertising by a significant margin. Where the most simple and least expensive TV spot ad will easily cost well over $50,000 and take months to produce, you can have a radio spot developed for less than $1,000 ... in a matter of days or weeks. In terms of media costs, you'll often pay a minimum of thousands of dollars for TV media placement. However, you can air a radio spot for under $100 at agency discounted rates and you can air a full week's radio advertising test on multiple stations for as little as $2,500. With TV, you can invest hundreds of thousands of dollars before you know whether a campaign will either take flight or until enough is learned to determine that it won't work. With radio, the testing happens much faster, so it costs you less in time value of money, as well as up-front and at-risk investment. Factor in TV dubbing costs, and the picture only gets better for radio.

Understanding Costs in Radio Advertising

There are two main cost "buckets" in radio advertising. One is the development of the ads themselves, or "creative development," as it is often called. The other cost is the airing of those ads, or the cost of media time.

Creative Development Costs

Because an ad has to be developed only once, that cost occurs once per ad and is relatively small (as we've mentioned, usually under $1,000 for a single-voice ad created by direct response radio experts). That same ad, if tests show it works well, will be aired many times; therefore, the larger cost over time is the media time.

Media Time Costs

The cost of media time is driven by a number of factors. The largest cost driver to air an ad on a radio station is the size of the audience. The more people you'll get exposure to, the more you'll pay. The second cost driver is the cost to reach each person—this is essentially the per-unit price the radio station puts on its product. Here it is necessary to introduce some basic radio advertising vocabulary. The size of the audience is a straightforward number usually obtained from Arbitron ratings reports. The cost per person you'll gain exposure to is called "CPM" which literally means "cost per thousand" and translates as "the cost in dollars to reach one thousand people." So, if you're looking to air an ad at a time of day that has 8,000 listeners on average (according to Arbitron figures) and the CPM is $5, you'll pay $40 per spot. The CPM differs across stations and dayparts, based on what the station thinks advertisers will pay. If there's more demand, as there often is during drive times, then the CPM will be higher. If you're buying a daypart that's either larger or deemed to have an audience of lesser "quality" (i.e., less likely to respond and buy or an audience with a lower percentage of the target demo you're after) the CPM will often be lower.

It's important to note that not all CPMs are created equal. A $5 CPM in Adults 12+ means virtually nothing to any advertiser. An advertiser whose target is Women 35–64 doesn't want to pay to reach the whole universe. The CPM will likely be somewhat higher with a narrowed demo, but the quality of that audience is higher because you aren't paying to reach people who aren't likely to buy your product.

Your radio agency will likely get you a significantly lower CPM than you could ever get on your own. This is due to a number of factors, including the longevity of the relationships your agency likely has with a large number of stations, the buying power your agency has as a result of having many clients (both in the past, the present, and the future), and the negotiating skills of your agency. On top of all of this, a good radio agency knows the most efficient schedules to book on your behalf, which will get you more results for every dollar you spend in advertising.

About Media Scheduling, Reach, and Frequency

To round out your practical understanding of how radio advertising works, it is helpful to have a basic understanding of two other terms. Let's first establish a "unit" of media time. In the case of direct response radio, it is common to buy a "schedule" of sixty-second airings that can be looked at as a series of one-week periods (for any number of weeks). Each one-week schedule will typically consist of a certain number of airings—usually more than ten and fewer than fifty—across different times of the day and days of the week.

The largest factors driving the cost of that schedule will be the *number of people* reached and *number of times* each person is reached. The former is called "reach," which is defined as *the number of different people exposed at least once to the ad over a specific period of time.* The metric of reach excludes duplication.

The average number of times a person is exposed to the ad during the one-week schedule is referred to as "frequency." Frequency can also be calculated by daypart for a particular one-week schedule, which is sometimes beneficial.

Reach and frequency are two sides of the same media coin. They are related because for any given dollar amount spent on a one-week media schedule, you can either try to expose as many people as possible to your ad (maximize reach), or you can try to expose those you do reach as many times as possible (maximize frequency). If the media dollar spend is held constant, maximizing frequency will reduce reach and vice versa. Typically you'll want to start testing with a frequency around three and then conduct further testing to identify the optimum reach and frequency (as well as other scheduling elements) for a specific campaign.

4. Radio Campaigns are Flexible and Scalable Profit Engines

Put simply, once you conclude testing with radio advertising, you have essentially created a growth engine for your business. And since it's direct response, you also have a nice dashboard of daily performance metrics to guide your business decision making. Therefore, you can grow your business at whatever rate and to whatever size you choose just by changing the amount of dollars you invest in the media spending.

CHAPTER 4

The Three Phases of Building a Direct Response Radio Campaign

> The work of an advertising agency is warmly and immediately human. It deals with human needs, wants, dreams and hopes. Its 'product' cannot be turned out on an assembly line.
>
> —Leo Burnett, *quoted in 100 LEO's*

Before going further, it will be helpful for you to have a macro perspective on the process for building direct response radio campaigns. We like to break it down in two ways.

The first way is a linear, chronological perspective that breaks the process into three phases:

- Strategy & Planning
- Testing & Refinement
- Rollout & Optimization

The second way to break down the process for building a direct response radio campaign is to look at the activities involved. This list is actually very long if you count every single activity, but in general there are six activities that take place in the building and optimization of a direct response radio campaign. They are:

- Planning
- Creative Development
- Testing
- Media Buying
- Results Data Analysis and Interpretation
- Campaign Profitability Optimization

The following table brings both of these perspectives together, showing the three phases along with the activities that take place in each one.

The Three Phases	Corresponding Activities
Phase One: Strategy & Planning	Planning, Creative Development, Media Planning, Testing Design
Phase Two: Testing & Refinement	Media Buying, Data Evaluation, Media and Creative Refinement
Phase Three: Rollout & Profitability Optimization	Media Buying, Ongoing Testing, Creative Development, Campaign Profitability Management

In the following few chapters we will address the major elements of the process of building a profitable direct response radio advertising campaign—the essentials of strategy development, creative development, media buying, testing, and profitability optimization.

CHAPTER 5

Developing Your Radio Advertising Strategy

The business world is particularly plagued by shoddy language. Employees and customers are inundated with jargon and "ad-speak," moribund clichés and windy phrases that signify nothing and are forgotten even before they are remembered.

–Dr. Frank Luntz, *Words That Work*

In phase one, the focus is on strategy and planning. The word "strategy" gets thrown around in so many different contexts that we've found it to have little real meaning when we are in discussions with clients. These words from Michael Porter,[v] one of the most respected management thinkers, can provide a clearer picture of what we need to accomplish when we develop a radio advertising strategy:

"Strategy is about making choices, trade-offs; it's about deliberately choosing to be different."

"...only strategy can create sustainable advantage. And strategy must start with a different value proposition. A strategy delineates a territory in which a company seeks to be unique. Strategy 101 is about choices: You can't be all things to all people."

"The essence of strategy is that you must set limits on what you're trying to accomplish. The company without a strategy is willing to try anything."

"If all you're trying to do is essentially the same thing as your rivals, then it's unlikely that you'll be very successful. It's incredibly arrogant for a company to believe that it can deliver the same sort of product that its rivals do and actually do better for very long. It's extremely dangerous to bet on the incompetence of your competitors..."

Porter was speaking about corporate competitive strategy, but the fundamental points he's making are very applicable to direct response advertising strategy. To be successful, you must a) be different, and b) not define yourself as the magical product or service that offers every possible benefit for nearly everyone. But these are difficult things to do. Why? Well, being different means trying what hasn't been tried, or doing what hasn't been done without any example to follow. That's risky and most people are risk averse. Another reason strategy is difficult is because it entails making choices. Trade-offs among many alternatives. As Barry Schwartz shows us in his popular book *The Paradox of Choice*, we perceive the opportunity cost of all the foregone options cumulatively, which hinders the kinds of decision-making processes in strategy development (and at the Chinese restaurant with a hundred choices on the menu).

For example, if your product can provide five different benefits to potential customers, you'll undoubtedly want to promote all five in your advertising. However, promoting just one or two of them is better. So first you have the challenge of choosing just two and discarding three.

Successful radio advertising campaigns require that certain fundamental pieces of information about the product (or service), customers, and business be clearly understood by everyone involved in the effort. Sales, marketing, customer service, and the agency should all have the chance to provide input from their perspectives, and all of these groups should be operating with the same complete set of information.

Without this foundation of common understanding, the chances of your radio advertising campaign being successful are diminished. Why? Because you slip from a methodical, disciplined approach to building your business profitably with direct response radio advertising to a more haphazard and risky approach that relies too much on luck. The way to business success with direct response radio is paved by discipline. The questions below are to be answered as part of just such a disciplined approach and they are meant to be addressed during the strategy phase of building your radio advertising campaign.

In many respects, building a successful direct response radio advertising campaign requires a mentality akin to that of a researcher. Researchers uncover knowledge about a particular topic. The first step in research is identifying the *big* questions you are trying to answer. In the case of direct response radio advertising, you are trying to answer the following *big* questions:

- Creative: which advertising appeals will result in *the highest number* of *most-qualified* leads?
- Media: which target audiences are *most responsive* to the product's advertising appeals *relative to the cost* of reaching them?

Answering these two *big* questions will minimize your media CPO, thereby maximizing your radio advertising (and overall business) profitability.

Ten Questions to Guide You to a Winning Radio Advertising Strategy

The list of questions that follows is aimed at guiding any potential radio advertiser down the road to revealing the answers to the *big* questions. The answers to the following questions are the input into creating and testing a hypothesis (again, thinking like a researcher) about which combination of radio advertising appeals and radio media targeting will result in the most profitable radio advertising campaign.

Note: we'll use the word "product"; however, the following thought process is also applied to services, events, and other items that are promoted in direct response radio advertising campaigns.

Product Questions

1. What benefits does the product provide to its users? What problems does it solve? In what ways does the product make the user's life better? Identify key claims that can legally be made about the degree of benefits to the product user. Specify all "reasons to believe" for each benefit. If relevant, describe how the product works.

2. Who are the product's competitors? Describe their current promotional strategy—which benefits are they promoting in their ads? What offers are they currently promoting? Any particularly relevant positioning or advertising tactics?

3. How is the product different? Be sure to compare the product to alternatives or substitutes, as well as to competing products. Also include information about any patents, trademarks, or clinical test results.

4.   What offers may be used in the radio advertisement? For example, is there a free trial, free shipping, or a bonus quantity with purchase?

5.   What are the distribution channel(s) that will be used for the product (Web, retail, direct)?

6.   Are customer testimonials, expert endorsements, or a corporate spokesperson available for use in the radio ad? This is important information because sometimes the most authentic appeal comes from existing customers or someone with the company who strongly believes in the product.

Customer Questions

Answering the following questions requires at least some customer research. It may be primary research (for example, conducting a qualitative focus group or a quantitative survey), or secondary research (reviewing qualitative or quantitative research compiled by others about your product category that you can apply to your specific situation). Don't overlook your current customer base and results from prior tests as sources of valuable customer information, but be aware that this data will not be randomly collected (i.e., to a large degree your current customers will be a reflection of the advertising that brought them in). In any case, research will not spell out the exact appeals that will be successful for your specific direct response radio advertising campaign, which is why in-market testing occurs in the next phase.

7. Who is in the target consumer segment? Describe them in terms of age, sex, socioeconomic, demographic, geographic, or other relevant dimensions.

8. What are the key consumer insights? What are the strongest motivations for this customer segment to buy this type or class of product? What does the customer hope to gain by purchasing, and what loss would the customer avoid by purchasing?

9. What objections or excuses might the customer use to delay or avoid buying the product? What is the answer to each of the objections or excuses?

Business Question

10. How will you measure success? What is your break-even media CPO (cost per order)? Armed with this information, you'll have a context with which to view the results of advertising tests. Without it, you are in

danger of either pulling the plug on a profitable campaign or rolling out an unprofitable campaign.

Once you've answered these questions, your agency is armed with the inputs it needs to develop a successful testing plan for your campaign.

CHAPTER 6

The Ten Characteristics of the Best Direct Response Radio Ads

"At the heart of an effective creative philosophy is the belief that nothing is so powerful as an insight into human nature, what compulsions drive a man, what instincts dominate his action, even though his language so often camouflages what really motivates him."

"There are two attitudes you can wear: that of cold arithmetic or that of warm, human persuasion. I will urge the latter on you. For there is evidence that in the field of communications the more intellectual you grow, the more you lose the great intuitive skills that make for the greater persuasion—the things that really touch and move people."

—William Bernbach, *quoted in Bill Bernbach said . . .*

The process of creating radio ads starts with a brainstorming of possible alternatives, and then is narrowed down into a short list of approaches that you hypothesize, based on sound rationale that will produce the best results. This part of the creative development is a challenging phase because it entails dealing with a large amount of information and a large number of potential alternatives. Plus, identifying appeals is only the first step—articulating those appeals is also very important—and nuanced. Often changing just two or three words can make a meaningful difference in the performance of an ad.

We strongly recommend that you define success of radio creative (radio ads) in terms of profitability, not popularity, awards won, or entertainment value. In our view, only one of these issues matters: Does the ad elicit response in the form of cost per lead (CPL) and cost per order (CPO) that results in the client acquiring the greatest number of profitable new customers? Stated differently, the goal of the ad is to persuade—persuade the listener to take an action that leads to a sale. The ad is not meant to please or entertain anybody. Just persuade.

With that in mind, we have distilled a list, in order of importance, of the top ten keys to creating great radio ads:

10. Production value and voice-over talent

Contrary to popular belief, production value and voice-over talent are not the most important elements in great radio ads. Yet they are what clients often use to determine whether they "like" an ad. From the data we've collected through eight years of testing radio ads, we've found that there is very often an inverse relationship between production value and ad performance. Yes, that's counterintuitive. Production value shouldn't "hurt" response, right? Wrong. There are a number of possibilities for why this is true.

Maybe focusing on a certain level of production value distracts ad developers from the right amount of attention on great copywriting.

Or, perhaps good production value creates an ad that is so "slick" that it doesn't stand out. As Seth Godin puts it, "perfect is boring." And as we know, boring doesn't sell.

Nonetheless, production and voice talent are still important. They simply need to be aimed at the right goal. Production must enhance believability, catch attention, and ensure the message can be ingested by the audience with minimal effort. The voice talent's read must be evaluated for its nonverbal communication, not just what the words mean as they're strung together.

When developing a radio ad, we focus on one element in particular when it comes to voice-over and production value: authenticity. "Great" voice-overs and super high-end production value can backfire if they are so "perfect" that they don't sound real. Fake turns people off. Therefore, in the production phase of an ad, what matters most is that the ad sounds real. That is not to say "real" as in a real radio ad, rather "real" as in a real person expressing real thoughts and feelings in a truthful, authentic way.

9. Degree of distinctiveness

The greater the me-too factor, the lower the potential for the campaign. For example, if your product is another of the hundreds of weight loss products or special diets, then you're likely going to have a difficult time coming up with something new to say to people. A lot of what can be said has been said. There is saturation because it's a me-too category. That doesn't mean it's not an opportunity. It's a huge category, but entering it without something very new would not be wise. Distinctiveness applies not just to the product benefits, but also to the creative approach, the offer, and any other element of the campaign and customer experience.

8. Effective use of the interplay between emotion and logic

Few purchase decisions, if any, are made based solely on logic or emotion alone. They are almost always a combination of the two. Therefore, there are points in the ad where emotional appeals are appropriate, and there are other points in the ad where logical appeals are potent. Quite often people are "reeled in" with emotion, and just before we buy we look for a logical reason to rationalize our emotional decision. Sound familiar? That's because it's one of those universal human characteristics. Successful radio ads recognize this and flow accordingly.

7. Articulation

There are a number of different ways to express your message. Anyone can get the message across. But there is only one optimum formula that presents the combination to the lock on the door of your customers' minds. Changing just one word or a few words in an ad can have an amazingly large impact on results. We've seen this over and over again—some key insight that produces a small copy change that dramatically boosts results. Or the opposite. Articulation matters. One of the biggest mistakes we've seen is using wishy-washy, non-specific language. Saying something like "Product A is designed to do X" is not as strong as saying "Product A does X." Another mistake is long sentences and pretentious words that talk over your customers. Keep sentences short, pointed, and simple—and don't try to win writing awards from the *New York Times*. The last time we checked, they don't send any money.

6. Simplicity

Yes, you love your product. You think it's the best thing in the history of the world. You can recount all of its amazing features and how each feature benefits every living human (and some not yet born) in fifty different ways. You are "drinking the Kool-Aid." We get it.

But if you try to convey all of the things anyone could ever love about your product in a radio ad, you will fail. You are making a classic mistake—a lack of strategy (see Chapter 5). In a one-minute radio ad, you have only sixty seconds to convince the people hearing the ad to take an action. Packing too much into the ad overwhelms the listener, triggering that natural cognitive process that minimizes sensory overload. What happens when the human brain is overwhelmed with too much information? It automatically looks for a shortcut. We experience this as a focusing moment—we block out everything and look for one cue that tells us what we need to know. That's it.

If people block out your ad, it will not produce good results. So don't put too many benefits in your ad. Focus on the most compelling benefit and the offer. If the sheer *number of benefits* is what's so impressive about your product or service, then at least test a focused approach next to that benefit "shotgun" so you can learn which performs better.

5. Use of sound elements to enhance the message and capture attention

We've separated this from #10 because we're not talking about a slick production value, rather the use of a specific production *technique* that introduces an element of surprise or discontinuity that helps the ad *stand out*. Sound elements that enhance ads are those that a) are not typical, b) are at least a little surprising and unpredictable, c) are not annoying, and d) are relevant to the ad and/or the product.

Integrating sound elements can't be done with maximum effectiveness as an add-on at the end of the production process. Use of sound elements should be considered as the ad is written; the use of sound that is irrelevant or detracts from the believability of the spot will hurt ad performance.

This is radio. It's called "the theater of the mind." But it doesn't have the limitations of a stage. In TV and print and other visual mediums, you can communicate visually with your audience. In radio, you need to "show" the audience a picture with sounds. It's both a burden and a benefit of radio advertising because it's harder to do but more impactful when done well. It's a burden on the copywriters because the words used to convey the message have a significant impact. But it's a blessing because the limitations are fewer. For example, if you want to show a picture of someone feeling happy in a TV ad, you need to find b-roll (video footage) or shoot original footage of just the right person. Are they male or female? What age? What ethnicity? Inside or outside? Moving or still? Summer or fall? With radio, you simply say "imagine the feeling..." and your audience—whoever they are—will create the perfect, personalized happy place that you are conjuring. There are no limitations in the imagination.

The most common mistake that is made with regard to sound in radio ads is the use of music. People very often assume that since it's a radio ad—and radio plays music—the ad "should" have music in the background. This is a horribly incorrect assumption, which—by the way—is reinforced by the radio stations themselves.

First of all, the majority of the best-performing ads we've seen have not had any background music. Second, we've tested this question many times—the same ad with and without background music. In only 11% of the cases, the ads with music have done better. After evaluating the results from our tests, we believe the music often interferes with the listeners' processing of the words or word meanings in the ad. Sometimes this is due to the relative volume of the music to the voice-over. In other cases, the music distorts the pronunciation of the words. For example, the high tones in the music match with highs in the pronunciation of words in the ad, requiring more focused listening to understand what's being said. This would hurt ad performance.

4. Authenticity

Authenticity is influential, believable, and enhances credibility. The best radio ads flow from an authentic connection to a product or service's uniqueness, the passion that created it, and the identity that it takes in the world. Authenticity is perhaps the most purely influential element an ad can convey.

It is also a differentiator, because most ads are not authentic.

Why? Because we're so conditioned to look outside ourselves and our businesses for clues about how to succeed. For example, many businesspeople develop an idea about what their ad should sound like by listening to other radio ads. That perspective gets injected into the creative process and ultimately replicated to at least a small degree, resulting in a me-too ad that doesn't do well.

Much more powerful ads come from tapping into the soul of a business and a product. The reason for being. The feelings, hopes, and fears that are aroused. This is difficult in our business environment because within companies, conformity is valued over true authenticity, and the result is that people say what they think others want to hear. Say what the boss wants to hear. Say what the customers want to hear.

But successful radio advertisers manage to reach beyond that fear and conditioning and speak from a place that is raw and true. Go there to find your authentic voice and you will be different.

3. The offer

As with nearly any direct response advertisement, there must be a call to action (CTA) that is relevant, compelling, and simple enough to grasp quickly. Relevant means it matters to a potential customer—it reduces my risk, makes picking up the phone a no-brainer, or gives me a reason to go with my emotions instead of my logic. Compelling means it has a "wow" factor. As in, "Wow, they must really believe in their product to do that." And simple means it's ... not complicated. It doesn't require the listener to think too much. It doesn't confuse the listener with language that's spun to sound like it's a great offer but really isn't.

One insight is pivotal here: the business model must be built with the potential offers in mind. Think about it—you can't make an offer in an ad that you can't afford to deliver on with your business. If you try this, you may get customers in the door, but you'll also lose them very quickly.

The CTA usually incorporates the response mechanism, which is typically a phone number or Web URL. One vital piece of advice: make sure the last sound of the ad is this phone number or Web URL. Resist the temptation to put another pithy slogan at the end, or worse, to insert legal disclaimer jargon there. The proper place for legal disclaimers is incorporated into the ad. The last sound should always be the URL or phone number (which should nearly always be repeated three times in succession at the end of the ad).

2. The opening attention grabber

The first impression of a great radio ad must provoke a desire for further exploration. If not, the radio ad will be categorized by the brain as the same old noise it always hears. And it will be blocked out—a victim of the cognitive processes that ensure we don't experience sensory overload. The challenge of grabbing attention is huge. Don't underestimate it. This is a difficult thing to do. Why? Because we're all bombarded relentlessly by a huge number of other advertisers who are trying to do it. And as we've pointed out, many people are copying other people, so lots of the ads look and sound like lots of others.

One way to think about the opening attention grabber is "don't bury the lead." Make sure the most impactful aspect of your ad is expressed early on. Get right to the point. You have sixty seconds to convince the listener to take action. Don't wait until twenty seconds into the ad to make your first unique, bold, relevant point. Make it within seven seconds or don't bother.

1. Benefit orientation

One of the biggest mistakes made in creating a radio ad is assuming people care *how something works* before they care what it *does for them*. You must say *how* only if the *what* is so incredible that you need a "reason to believe" in the ad—and then you do it in one sentence or less.

A great radio ad always answers the question that is top of mind for every single human listening: *What's in it for me?* How will it impact my life in a way that I think will make my life better, happier, or easier?

This requires understanding and tapping into the fundamental human beliefs around these topics. For example, do people care about a product that prevents a problem they don't yet have? No. They think, "I don't care about that. I have these ten problems right now; why would I worry about something I don't even have yet?" Current problems matter more than potential future problems. Prevention doesn't sell.

What sells is something that convinces people it'll solve a problem quickly, safely, better, and more conveniently than anything else. If you use your sixty seconds in any other way than to tell this story, you're wasting your time—and your money.

CHAPTER 7

The #1 Key to Understanding Profitable Radio Media Buying

It is not necessary to advertise food to hungry people, fuel to cold people, or houses to the homeless.

—John Kenneth Galbraith, *American economist*

Whole books have been written on the topic of media buying. It is perhaps the most technical and complex aspect of building successful radio advertising campaigns because it entails working with a combination of many variables. As such, it requires not only the support of robust technology but also the acumen that can be developed only over years of experience in specific radio advertising situations, product and service categories, and geographic markets. We'll not repeat here what those tomes on media buying already cover. Not only are they long, they're also often more theoretical than experiential. Theory is great for the academic, but for those of us who need to put points on the board in real-life business situations, the learnings from direct experience are more valuable, practical, and informative.

Therefore we'll focus on the key insight you need to understand how media buying works in direct response radio advertising when it's done right.

While the creative development of radio ads is concerned almost solely with developing the "right message," the media-buying aspect of building direct response campaigns is concerned with getting that right message to the **right people** at the **right place and time** for the **right cost.**

This is a very important statement to understand because it tells us that:

a) Success does not result from getting the right message to the right people at the right place and time for *too high a cost.*

b) Success does not result from getting the right message to the wrong people at the wrong place and time for *the lowest cost.*

Many people approach radio with a "get me the lowest rates" mentality. They ask about getting the biggest discount or talk about getting remnant (unsold inventory) rates. But when you understand the above statements, you can see that effective direct response media buying is not solely about how much you pay. How much you pay for the airtime is, of course, important. The confusion seems to arise when there's a focus on cost to the exclusion of the other elements we've highlighted. When you execute on all of these is when you see amazingly profitable campaigns.

Similarly, we've heard many people say, "I *have* to be in morning drive," or "I have to be in afternoon drive." It's understandable that an intelligent businessperson wants to ensure the media buy is appropriately crafted to reach the "right people," but there is still confusion here about the interplay among the elements required for successful media buying. It's not that black and white.

Requiring a certain daypart does not take into account the cost of that daypart. Remember, *it's what you get for what you pay.* Airing in morning drive may deliver a large number of your customers, but if it comes at too high a cost, then it doesn't matter that you've reached your customers. The experienced direct response radio agency has gained the skills, knowledge, and relationships necessary to procure the kind of media schedules that deliver profitable outcomes. And they may not look the way someone schooled in classical marketing principles would expect them to.

Which leads us to the key insight:

> Effective direct response radio media buying is about *what you get for what you pay*. Paying $1 to reach the wrong people at the wrong place and time is not worth $1, as cheap as that is.Likewise, paying $2,500 to reach adults twenty-five to fifty-four on morning drive in Los Angeles is very likely not worth it if you get only eighty calls, ten orders, and $1,000 in lifetime revenue.

When it comes to media buying, you won't get away with doing only one part of it well. Getting your message to the right people is a vital driver of success for your campaign. Reaching the wrong people with your message at any cost and at any place and time is purposeless. Whether they are wrong because they don't want your product, or wrong because they're not the customer segment you're after, the wrong people will not produce the right results. Likewise, paying too much will negate even the most well-targeted media buys.

Arriving at "The Right Cost"

Much of successful media buying distills into knowing how much to pay to air a spot or schedule of spots on a particular radio station or network. There are a number of ways to approach media buying. We'll use one basic approach here for illustration.

To arrive at the right cost—that is, the right rate to pay for a given spot airing—you begin with an appropriate cost per lead (CPL) target. This target is arrived at based on a review of both the profitability characteristics of each individual campaign and what is deemed achievable based on prior experience in the same or similar categories and situations.

From there it is possible to "back into" a media rate that yields that targeted CPL. The knowns in this mathematical process are: cost, audience size, and number of leads. That means the only unknown (for this simplified example) in this process is the responsiveness of the particular station's audience. In essence, this is a measure of audience quality. This is where direct response techniques come into play. One immense benefit of combining the database techniques of direct marketing with radio advertising is that it becomes possible to gain an understanding over time of the response characteristics of individual stations, networks, markets, and formats across all product categories and creative approaches. With this knowledge, the appropriate response rate can be determined and applied to arrive at the "right cost."

What this all boils down to is a "pay for performance" scenario. In the realm of direct response advertising, the radio stations and networks are paid based on the value they bring to each individual campaign. That's why it pays for radio stations to focus first on audience quality, and second on audience size.

CHAPTER 8

Five Tips for Effective Testing

> To swear off making mistakes is very easy. All you have
> to do is swear off having ideas.
>
> –Leo Burnett

It would be very difficult to overstate the role and importance of testing in building successful direct response radio campaigns. At first, the idea of testing seems simple, even basic. Of course you have to test. You wouldn't just spend $100,000 behind an ad without first testing it.

But in direct response radio, testing runs much deeper than that. It's in the culture and the neural fibers of direct response organizations because testing almost never ceases. On some level, there is always testing occurring in a campaign. An understanding of the process of testing must therefore be woven throughout each phase of the campaign.

Additionally, testing is a sub-function of direct response that requires its own specialized skill set, namely an understanding of basic statistics and familiarity with the scientific method and field research.

We borrow a lot from the scientific method used in behavioral science because we must be able to a) set up a test correctly, b) capture the right data, and c) evaluate that data in a manner that ensures we're making accurate interpretations.

For clarification, the "scientific method" can be summarized as: *The principles and empirical processes of discovery and demonstration considered characteristic of or necessary for scientific investigation, generally involving the **observation** of phenomena, the formulation of a **hypothesis** concerning the phenomena, **experimentation** to demonstrate the truth or falseness of the hypothesis, and a **conclusion** that validates or modifies the hypothesis.* [vi]

Of course, unlike lab settings that most behavioral scientists applying the scientific method work in, direct response radio is more like field research—messy, complicated, and imperfect. Still, the alternative is a chaotic starting over at the beginning of the learning curve for each campaign, and even each ad copy.

Possibly there is no such thing as the scientific method, for "scientific" is a descriptive rather than a definitive term, and therefore applies to many methods. It implies carefulness, and patience, and thoroughness, and in general a very high type of workmanship. It requires both deduction and induction, both analysis and synthesis. –Edmund McGarry[vii]

Here are five tips for ensuring you receive the most benefit from testing.

1. Identify specifically what question you are trying to answer from a particular round of testing. Always keep the question in mind when making decisions throughout the testing phase. Because there are often many questions to address, it is very easy to lose sight of what you are trying to learn in a single round of testing, so take this very seriously, and do whatever you need to do to remain focused on these questions and ensure that the testing is set up to provide the best answers possible.

2. Test variables in order of most impactful to least impactful so each round of testing informs the following round. For example, if you are choosing

between testing whether to target men or women and testing whether you should say "improves" or "boosts," test the bigger-picture question of male or female first. Why? Because wording won't matter if you've written for the wrong target. Typically you will focus on questions such as which formats (media variable) and demographic targets (creative element) will produce the best results. Once you get a read on these big-picture test variables, you begin to test the other variables (like openings and offers), gradually working your way to the variables that tend to have a more subtle impact.

3. Don't change too many things at once. This is a big no-no. Ideally you will change only one variable at a time so you can attribute all of the difference in results to that change. In reality it can be difficult to change only one thing at a time—there may simply not be enough time or money. You may want to test a different format (media variable) and a different open (creative variable). You must know that the more you change at once, the less valuable the results will be. Do your best to resist this temptation within the business realities that confine testing (like limits on time and money).

4. Collect a big enough sample size of data. It would be nice if you could test one airing on one station

and be able to extrapolate those results to all stations. But that's not the way it works. You need a sample size big enough to make a reliable conclusion. How big? In general, the higher the variability in the data, the bigger the sample size. From a practical standpoint, we have found that testing one ad on five to ten stations across no more than two formats in about $5,000 of media is a minimum amount necessary to get a good read.

5. Define success correctly. What does failure look like in the testing phase? It's not lack of profitability. It's lack of learning. The goal of testing is to uncover and produce knowledge. Not to produce a profit. Done correctly, testing will lead you to the most profitable radio advertising campaign possible. Done incorrectly, you'll have spent money on radio advertising and still won't be able to draw any conclusions about what works and what doesn't for your campaign. Testing is a period of time you've carved out to plot your course through the universe of possible routes in direct response radio. If you don't take the time to plot that course as clearly as possible, your journey will be fraught with wrong turns and missed opportunities.

The last item to note here is that testing never actually stops in direct response radio. Even though you'll move into the rollout phase, testing will continue, just as a much smaller percentage of your total spending. This ongoing testing is vital, because effective radio ads have a finite life. They will tire out and need to be replaced with fresh creative. If you don't test when things are going great, you won't have ads ready to go when results from the control ad start to fade.

CHAPTER 9

On The Air: Eight Ways to Maximize Your Profits

> There is a great deal of advertising that is much better
> than the product. When that happens, all that the good
> advertising will do is put you out of business faster.
>
> –Jerry Della Famina,
> *From Those Wonderful Folks Who Gave You Pearl Harbor*

You've achieved a profitable CPO (advertising cost per order) in testing and now you're moving to phase three where you'll most likely want to grow the size of the radio campaign so you can grow your business. With this move, you'll need to keep an eye on profitability. We call this process profitability optimization. Profitability optimization is essentially the continuous improvement process that ensures you're reaping maximum profitability from direct response radio. Achieving rollout is a major milestone. It means you've achieved profitability. Even better than that, you've built a flexible, scalable profit engine for your business. As soon as you are on the air in rollout mode, there are a number of moving parts in the campaign that need to be maintained and improved.

The Basic Formula

In discussing profitability optimization, it's necessary to review the basic formula involved in all direct response advertising:

> You buy placement in radio media to air your radio ad, which gets your message broadcast to a certain number of people.
>
> Some percentage of those people who hear your message will respond (call, visit your Web site, visit your store), giving you a response rate.
>
> Of those who respond (otherwise known as leads), a percentage will be converted into customers (orders), and by that conversion rate generate profit and revenue.

From this formula, you will derive your media "CPO," or "cost per order," which is found by dividing media spend by the number of orders achieved with that spend (media spend in the numerator/number of orders in the denominator). This is the amount it costs you in radio advertising dollars to acquire one new customer, which is why it is also called "cost per acquisition" (CPA).

Assessing Your Profitability

The important question at this point is this: Is the lifetime value (LTV) of each of your customers, on average, positive given this CPO? That is, when you add up all the revenue from that customer, and you subtract all other costs (for example, cost of goods, credit card fees, fulfillment, sales), do you get a number that is greater than your advertising CPO? This fundamental question applies whether your business is a direct response advertising business (which includes radio advertising, print advertising, DRTV, catalog, or Internet) or a traditional retailer. Every business pays to acquire a customer (whether through a retail location, a sales force, an advertising campaign, or some combination thereof), and every business has a certain propensity and skill for retaining that customer over a period of time in a relationship consisting of subsequent purchases and therefore revenue (and hopefully profit) streams.

Regardless of whether your business uses direct response radio to acquire new customers, or uses one of the other approaches for customer acquisition, your success will be fundamentally based on whether your business model facilitates a strongly positive lifetime value. If it does not, there is little that radio advertising, or any other form of advertising, can do to change this.

If your LTV is not positive with your current CPO, you will remain in phase two and continue testing. Your business isn't profitable yet and you'll want to make the changes to both the advertising and the business model that will result in profitability.

Once you've achieved a CPO that works with your business to produce a positive LTV, you will want to increase the amount of profit per order to maximize your advantage. To do this, you'll need to increase revenues and/or improve your cost structure. This process is called business (or campaign) profitability optimization, and it is absolutely essential to the long-term success of any direct response radio advertising effort. Here are eight approaches (broken into two groups of four) to consider employing to increase your profit per order.

Increasing Your Revenues

There are a number of ways to increase the revenue stream from each customer. Let's look at the main ways of doing this:

1. Increase price without increasing cost. One way to do this is by increasing the percentage of orders that include higher-margin upsells. Retailers do this all the time. They put super-high-margin items right at the checkout. Direct response advertisers can learn a lot from this. Identify widely appealing, complementary items and ensure they are offered as part of the sales process.

2. Increase repeat purchases. You have paid to acquire those customers, now develop an ongoing relationship by continuing to meet customers' needs to drive repeat purchases. If they buy only once from you, you don't have a very viable business unless that single purchase delivers an incredibly high margin.

3. Reactivate former customers. Get them to come back to your business and restart a relationship

with them. The most likely targets are those who have purchased two or more times from you but have been inactive for thirty to sixty days.[viii]

4. Reduce your return rate. Often one of your biggest "leakages" of revenues will be the returns from customers who try your product or service and don't like it. Find out why, and address the issue. This is perhaps the best way to learn how to improve your business.

Improving Your Cost Structure

To improve cost structure in a direct response business, you can look at two distinct "buckets" of costs.

The first bucket is your non-advertising cost structure. This will be items such as your cost of sales, cost of goods, fulfillment, customer service, shipping, merchant fees, and returns and cancellations. In these areas, the most beneficial approach is to leverage your increased volume to negotiate better rates with each vendor. If you have vendors you were with when you began your campaign, you're likely a much bigger customer now than you were then. Losing you as a customer would be a big problem for them and it's very often worth it to them to reduce their margin to keep a larger customer rather than spend cash to acquire a new (possibly risky) customer.

The second bucket of costs contains your advertising-related costs.

1. Reduce the media cost per impression of your message. Also known as CPM, this is a standard metric used in advertising. It reflects the cost to reach 1,000 sets of ears. (Remember that CPM stands for "cost per thousand" impressions of your message). The process of reducing the cost of advertising is a constant focus of any good direct response radio agency. The agency is highly motivated to get the lowest possible CPM, while not giving up quality of airtime, because this results in a larger and longer-lasting business relationship with the client—which is the most profitable scenario for a radio agency. In this way, the incentives and the client are well aligned. Every dollar of media in direct response radio is either highly discounted or left over unsold ("remnant") advertising. The other way to reduce CPM is to dial in on the optimum schedule for a particular format and station. Optimizing the media schedule can meaningfully reduce CPM. Your agency should be using database

technology and scientific testing to identify the optimum schedule.

2. Increase response rate. Again, media scheduling will play a role here. In addition, use of radio formats to effectively target the right customers is vital to optimizing response rate. But perhaps the greatest impact on response rate in direct response radio advertising is the messaging in the radio ad itself. Great direct response radio ads significantly enhance the response rate for the media dollars spent. Your radio agency's ability to create radio ads that elicit response from your potential customers is a crucial element in direct response radio advertising success.

3. Increase conversion rates. Increasing the percentage of inquiries that become customers can have an enormous impact on campaign profitability. The factors that will most impact conversion rate are your sales scripting, Web copy, product offers, pricing, and your guarantee or return policy. As much as any other variable, these factors need to be tested and continuously refined. Don't be afraid to test different sales vendors. We've seen a marked difference in sales conversions and average revenue per sale across different sales call centers.

4. Institute a non-buyer recovery program. If your conversion rate is 30%, that means for every order you get, you are receiving 2.3 leads who don't convert to buyers. Find out why they're not buying and develop a promotion tailored to the most attractive segment of non-buyers.

CHAPTER 10

Self Test: Are You Ready For Direct Response Radio?

"It takes a big idea to attract the attention of consumers
and get them to buy your product.
Unless your advertising contains a big idea,
it will pass like a ship in the night."

–David Ogilvy, *Ogilvy on Advertising*

The first step in "doing radio right" is not to do it until you're ready. The number one reason radio advertising hasn't worked for a business is that it hasn't been approached appropriately. It hasn't been "done right."

It seems a funny thing to be stating, but we're constantly surprised at how many businesses want to start advertising on radio before their business is prepared to conduct the effort in a manner that has the greatest chance of success.

When you start advertising on the radio, you're spending valuable dollars that must generate commensurate profits, and you're turning on an engine of business growth that will have implications for your business. You must be able to handle the situations that will arise when you begin to advertise. Otherwise, you will fail. And by fail, we mean you will spend money and get nothing for it—not revenue, not profit, and most importantly, not learning about what will and won't work for your business. So, as loudly and as clearly as we can say it, we're saying, "Don't begin a direct response radio advertising effort until you're ready!"

The questions presented here will help you determine whether you and your business are ready to begin with direct response radio advertising. If you're not ready, we'll tell you the steps you need to take to get ready.

Question #1: How will you define success?

Seems simple, right? Maybe you're saying, "Drive new leads." "Grow our profits." "Acquire new customers."

That's not good enough.

OK, you say, how about this. "Drive 100 new leads." "Grow our profits by 10%!" "Acquire twenty new customers."

Still not good enough. Why? Where did you get those numbers? Probably the same place most businesses get them. You ballpark. You ask, "What would my boss think would be a good answer—that's what I'll say." Not only is that hogwash (we all knew that already), it's also unnecessary because with direct response radio, you don't need to guess. It's all in the numbers.

Here's the question you need to answer first: How much, in profit, is each customer worth to your business over the course of that customer's relationship with your company? This figure is the customer lifetime value for your business and it is **vital** to know this before you go into direct response advertising.

Why is this vital to know? After all, lots of people don't know it, and they do OK, right? And it's also really hard to calculate. Do I really need to do it?

Yes, you do. Because the definition of success in direct response radio advertising is acquiring a new customer at a cost that allows for a profitable relationship with that new customer. If you don't know the lifetime value, you cannot know how much you are able to pay to acquire a customer. All of those people who don't know it and get away with it are either getting lucky or actually slowly going out of business without even knowing it. Our view about luck us this: Yes, "luck counts," but don't count on luck. Luck counts because you will get lucky sometimes and those profits "count." They are on your P&L and in your bank. But don't count on luck because you can't build a consistently profitable business—or direct response radio advertising campaign—on luck.

Think about the day when you run your first ad schedule on a station. The results come in. How do you know whether they are good or bad? Are they good because there is revenue? Are they good because the phone is ringing or because visits to the Web site went up? These are not sufficient to understand and evaluate the performance of your advertising. You can evaluate advertising performance only within the context of your customer lifetime value. And you must evaluate the performance of your advertising if you are going to earn a profit with it.

But knowing your customer lifetime value is not enough. You have to break this down into the metrics that you'll use to evaluate and manage your campaign. These metrics are part of the formula for lifetime value, metrics like "cost per lead" (CPL), cost per order (CPO, also known as CPA or cost per acquisition), conversion rate, and average revenue per sale. Do not begin a direct response radio advertising campaign (or a business of any sort using any kind of demand generation tactics) until you know your business profitability metrics very well. Business profitability modeling is beyond the scope of this book. What we will say here is that you must model your business in a way that reveals the revenue by type (various offer configurations or product lines) along with the corresponding cost structure. Obviously, revenue minus costs gives you some sort of profit figure, at least variable profit or gross margin. Typically this kind of modeling is done in an Excel spreadsheet, and the result shows you exactly how your business will behave under many different scenarios. This, in turn, allows you to not only evaluate your advertising, but also to make decisions with respect to maximizing your profitability—especially as it relates to providing your radio agency with the necessary information to maximize your return on advertising spending.

Question #2: Are you prepared to test?

We have often heard people say, "We tried radio advertising and it doesn't work for us."

Here's the problem with that statement: Developing a profitable direct response radio advertising campaign isn't something that is accomplished with a "trial." It is far too complicated an endeavor, with far too many variables, to assess its effectiveness for your business with a randomly approached "trial." There are creative variables and media variables, and together they present a daunting number of possible combinations to achieve success.

To properly assess the potential for direct response radio advertising to generate profitable new customers for your business, you must approach direct response radio advertising with a testing mindset. That calls for a patient, methodical approach, preferably infused with knowledge from someone who has climbed the radio advertising learning curve and can start you out way farther along than from the 0, 0 point.

What does this mean for you? It means that you need around $20,000 to develop and adequately test multiple ads over a four- to eight-week period before you'll know which approaches will (and won't) yield more profitable results. Don't go into direct response radio advertising with a "dabble" mindset. Go into it holding yourself accountable for meeting solid, productive business goals: a) to assess the potential of direct response radio advertising to drive profitable new revenues, and b) to understand which approaches—both creative and media—produce the best results for your company.

While you'll generate revenues and profits during the test, the real benefit of testing is in the learnings that can be applied to a larger campaign over a long period of time to drive significant sales and profits.

When we ask if you're prepared to test, what we mean is that testing is part of the nature of direct response advertising. It is where all of the initial knowledge about the path to success for your campaign is created. If you are not willing to test, then you are essentially gambling. Rolling the dice. You'll have to take shortcuts and hope that you "hit" on one of them. If you don't, you'll say, "We tried radio, and it didn't work for us." But you'll be deceiving yourself.

If, however, your mindset is, "I am going to conduct a test of radio advertising," and your goal is not to hit it by luck but rather by a reliable, replicable, methodical approach, then you will benefit. At the worst, the very worst case, you may find that radio does not meet your business requirements for customer acquisition cost. From that point forward, you can focus your energy elsewhere because you've fully and correctly answered a vital business question: "Is radio a viable avenue for profitable growth for my business?" When you answer that question after a thorough testing approach, you can move on without looking in the rearview mirror. Or, maybe at some point in the future you've improved your business in such a way that you've increased your customer lifetime value to a point where radio becomes a viable venue. Now you have the learnings from your test to look back on and a whole new way to grow your business.

Question #3: Do you have a compelling offer?

The offer in your direct response radio ad is one of the most important elements for success. But why do you need to be thinking about that before you even approach radio advertising? Isn't that something your radio advertising agency should come up with? Well, yes, but... The "but" here hinges on the fact that any offer must be something that's possible given the business profitability structure, and possible given the systems and processes that run the business. These are constraints that only you know about. It will take time to alter existing systems or processes should that be necessary to support a compelling offer in your advertising.

For example, your radio agency might recommend an offer such as a free DVD player with each order. That would drive a lot of orders, but would they be profitable? You need to define the playing field for the agency and then engage in the dialogue of getting the most out of what's possible given a) the business constraints and b) what the agency knows does and doesn't work in direct response radio advertising.

What is a compelling offer? It's different, it's relevant, and it's meaningful. A complimentary product or service is a good example. For example, if you're marketing a skin care product that fights acne, you can give away a skin softener product as a bonus. This qualifies as different if it's not the same thing that every other skin care product is offering. It's relevant because often acne products cause dry skin. It's meaningful because it has perceived value to the customer—it's not something you can get anywhere for free or really cheap.

Some campaigns use free trials. These work extremely well with products that deliver on their promises consistently and noticeably. Others use a combination of free trial with a conversion attempt at the point of sale. This means they advertise their free offer and attempt to upsell the customer to another offer. This requires a skilled call center and strict following of the rules. Still others employ the "risk-free trial" approach, which essentially positions the thirty-day money-back guarantee as an offer—a "risk-free trial." The offer possibilities are many, yet coming up with a different, relevant, and meaningful offer can be challenging and should be given plenty of time and attention.

Question #4: Is your business infrastructure set up to support direct response radio advertising?

The most important aspect of preparing for direct response radio advertising is ensuring you're ready for the volume of leads and orders that can result. The easiest way to project this is to know your CPL and CPO projections (see above) and then assume a specific weekly media spend. For example, say you're running $25,000 in media per week in direct response radio. This is considered a relatively small campaign. If your business model shows that you expect a CPL of $15, then you'll be driving 25,000/15 = 1,667 calls per week. Can your sales call center and fulfillment center handle this volume? More importantly, can they handle more, because when you're profitable while running a $25,000 weekly radio campaign, you'll undoubtedly want to grow to five to ten times that size as soon as possible.

There's another vital piece of infrastructure you absolutely must have in place before you begin direct response radio advertising. It is a firm requirement because without it you're wasting your money and ruining your reputation with the vendors you've hired to help you build the campaign. That requirement is excellent data collection and transmission to the radio media buying department at your radio agency. This is because data analysis is how you determine the results of your testing, and close evaluation of the data is how your radio agency produces the insights about what does and doesn't work for your specific campaign—the very insights that can mean the difference between wild success or opportunity missed.

This means that you absolutely must have a mechanism for capturing the lead, order, and revenue data by the unique identifier (such as the toll-free phone number) for the media buy that generated the call. If you're sending calls to an experienced direct response call center, this is no problem. They understand this need and are already set up to accommodate it. If you're trying to take calls in-house, most of the time you've got work to do to ensure you can provide your radio agency with the information needed on a timely basis (no later than first thing every morning for the previous day's data). If you are sending leads to a Web site, which is happening with increasing frequency, you must set up data capture and transmission mechanisms via a Web tracking software program like Google Analytics before the campaign begins, preferably before you even contact a direct response radio advertising agency to get started. It's amazing how many times we've been told that this tracking mechanism is in place and that we'll get daily data exports from the Web tracking software, only to begin the test and find out either that we won't be receiving data for many days, if ever, or that what we do receive will not be complete. Or both.

Lack of data collection and timely transmission to your radio agency doesn't work in direct response radio. You may as well not start.

Question #5: Are you aware of your biases and assumptions?

This question probably sounds a little different than the rest but it's well worth spending some time on. What you must understand is that you, the client, lead the show. As the agency, we will tell you what we recommend based on our expertise in the field of direct response radio advertising. However, you, as the client, have an important responsibility that must be met for success to result. It's up to you to make sure we're making our recommendations with all of the necessary information. Biases and assumptions, as much as incomplete information, can damage this important aspect of the client-agency relationship.

Biases and assumptions underlie beliefs you have about key campaign questions like why your customers buy from you or what appeals in advertising will resonate with the target audience. If you inject these into the process as facts, your agency will likely take them as such. The agency is unlikely to argue strongly with you—it's just the nature of the "the customer is always right" tendency in client-agency relationships (as well as many others).

Let's say you've been advertising online with banners and pay per click (or with TV or with print—the medium doesn't matter). You want to test radio. One common mistake is to do a survey of your existing customers and ask them why they buy. The results show that the reasons these people buy are A, B, and to a lesser degree, C. You conclude that the exact same approach will work in radio and you require that approach be followed by the agency. But you've made a big mistake. You've overlooked the fact that your survey was very biased. Why? Because the people you surveyed were prompted to become customers by the ads you ran. Of course their reasons for buying will match up very well with the appeals in the advertisements that you've been running. You're always going to find that existing customers validate the ads you've run—they responded to them to become customers! The unbiased way to do a survey is to collect data from a random sample of at least thirty people (not current customers) matching the target customer profile.

Notice the point is not to eradicate your biases or assumptions, but to become aware of them. It's nearly impossible to get rid of biases. However, if you're aware of them you can then test them methodically and you won't be in danger of leading your agency down the wrong path—one that often leads to the failure of radio campaigns. If you reveal your biases to your agency, the agency can determine the most appropriate way to handle them in the context of your initial testing.

Question #6: Are you different?

Me-too products or services don't work, period. In some marketing efforts you find this out over a period of months or quarters. In direct response you find this out very quickly. You must be different. First of all, different captures attention, and you must have attention before you get action—or response. Secondly, among the sea of products offered, you must be different in the benefits you offer to solve the problem that others are also purporting to solve.

One important insight about "different" is that you can be different in any one of a number of possible ways. Brett recalls a certain marketing professor at the University of Michigan who liked to point out that "you can innovate anywhere in the value chain...the more places the better."

For example, did Dell Computer make innovative new computers? Not at all. This should surprise you—after all, what business is Dell in? If their computers weren't different, then what accounts for the enormous financial success of the company? The answer is: multifaceted differentiation in many places along the value chain (the value chain is the "chain" of activities that comprise the entire business a company is involved in).

Dell is perhaps best known for innovation in distribution within the computer industry—the "Dell direct model." When nobody thought it was possible to sell a computer to someone who couldn't first see and touch it, Dell went ahead and sold computers by catalog and then the Web, shipping them directly to customers. And made a killing. Dell also found a way to put computers together faster (different assembly approach), achieve higher computer reliability (different in quality), and to do so at a lower cost (different cost structure) than any other PC maker. These things, among others, translated into a super-low-cost structure, which meant Dell could beat competitors on price and still make more money than those competitors.

Then, Dell figured out a way to reduce inventory (different operations management) by configuring the assembly plants in a certain way. Additionally, Dell worked out payment terms with vendors that allowed them to pay vendors well after Dell had received payments from customers (different financial structure). These differentiators resulted in reduced working capital, thereby boosting Dell's return on invested capital while reducing cost of debt. The effects of these moves produced multifaceted advantages throughout the company. The list for Dell could continue, but the point here is made: Dell did not innovate in the product it produced (as has Apple, for example)...nor did Dell innovate so much in its marketing or advertising—it didn't need to. All it had to do was promote its low price.[ix]

There are other, perhaps less extreme, examples of differentiation. Maybe you're marketing a product in the diet aid category. There are "support" food programs (Weight Watchers), pills (TRIMSPA) and informational/diet regimens (the Atkins diet). Do you have to have the latest breakthrough pill to compete? That would be nice but there are only so many of those to be discovered. So you can be different in another way. Your spokesperson could be a celebrity. Your marketing angle could be radically different. Your offer could be unique. Your cost structure or overall business model might allow for an incredible free gift or a very low price. Your customer retention program might be so strong that you can give away a free trial to acquire large numbers of customers. There are many, many ways to be different.

How you're different—while important—is still second to the fact that if you're a me-too product or if you have a me-too advertising message, you'll not last long.

CHAPTER 11

Final Warning: The Four Biggest Mistakes in Direct Response Radio

Rarely have I seen any really great advertising created without a certain amount of confusion, throwaways, bent noses, irritation and downright cursedness.

— Leo Burnett, *100 LEO's*

So far we've approached this book by revealing the inside tips vital for understanding and applying direct response radio advertising to grow business profits. This chapter takes a different approach by revealing the top mistakes we've seen. You can interpret these as the five most damaging mistakes we most often encounter on the way to building successful campaigns.

Biggest Direct Response Radio Mistake #4: Faulty or Nonexistent Testing Methodology

There are many ways for a testing methodology to fall short, which is why this is on the list. Testing the wrong variables, testing in the wrong order, testing too many variables, testing too few variables. The list is long. The point to remember is that success requires a scientific approach. That means disciplined and well thought out—a "ready, aim, fire" approach versus "fire, fire, fire." A good direct response agency has a staff that understands the process for conducting scientific research, particularly research methods, statistics, and database management. The best direct response agencies have applied this knowledge to many campaigns over time and as a result have developed a *proven* testing methodology that yields the quickest and most reliable results. They have the supporting technological infrastructure that will get you from testing to profitability with the least amount of up-front time and money.

If you don't follow a well-defined, proven testing methodology, you are throwing your ad dollars away. Period. You simply will not know why—or even whether one ad works better than another or whether there are other approaches that could work better. You will just be out of money before you can determine whether your campaign has legs.

Biggest Direct Response Mistake #3: Not Capturing the Data

The power of direct response radio stems in large part from the ability to collect and evaluate results from the bounty of data that can be collected—and from that process to distill insights that drive further refinement of the campaign. As all experienced marketers know, it is the insights that lead you through the dark forest of possibility onto the well-lit path to success.

In direct response, you are driving leads in some kind of measurable way. Typically those leads are directed to a call center or a Web site or both. Often they are directed to a retail site. Regardless of where the leads are directed, you *must* ensure a system is in place to capture the lead, order, and revenue data, *and* to transmit the data to your radio agency in a timely fashion. Your call center, web management firm or store management must assist with this process. In the case of call centers and web management companies, tracking and reporting data is a standard part of their service offering (provided they're appropriate service providers for direct response campaigns. If they're not, you shouldn't use them. See mistake #2).

Yet many times this process does not get executed. We have too often been promised by a client that the data capture element is in place only to find—after the ads have been aired initially—that we won't be receiving data, or that the data we will get is to be delayed and incomplete.

Biggest Direct Response Mistake #2: Fielding a Poor Team

In most cases, you're going to assemble a team of vendors to help execute your direct response radio campaign. The core members of direct response teams are similar for many campaigns. There is the manufacturer or service-delivery company, the fulfillment company, the sales and customer service entity, and the creative and media agency. Your selection of vendors will contribute heavily to your success. Don't choose a buddy's company or the local call center if they aren't deeply experienced in direct response radio—specifically. Realize this: all the vendors you talk to will say they can do what you are looking for. Many of them have very good salespeople. Take your time, ask for—and talk to—many references, and get to know the people at companies, not just the sales representatives. Remember, if everything goes as planned, you will be spending a lot of time working with these vendors. They must be team players without big egos. If not, you'll have more headaches than you can count.

Biggest Direct Response Mistake #1: A Corrupted Creative Process

There are many mistakes that can be made during the creative process. One of the most common is hurrying. A curiously high percentage of clients approach us in a big hurry to get on the air. As the agency, we want to do everything we can to make that happen. The reality can be, though, that we rush the strategy and creative process. The creative process itself requires time. Understanding why requires an understanding of what human creativity is. In short, it's not logical or linear. It requires space and clarity for the gestation of ideas. Rushing that process can undermine the quality of the output.

Another mistake is asking your agency to create an ad that would sell *you* (the client) on buying (even though *you* aren't the target or a large enough sample size to extrapolate from). Similarly, guiding your agency toward creating an ad that makes you feel proud, one you'll feed good about sending to your friends (even though *they* aren't the target) is a mistake. Why? Because very rarely is an ad designed with this orientation the same kind of ad that will produce

CPLs (cost per lead) and CPOs (cost per order) that result in a profitable direct response advertising campaign.

You've got to very clearly communicate one thing to your direct response agency: how do you as the client define success? Agencies, after all, want to please the client. If you ask for an ad that will make you happy then you'll get exactly that. Likewise, if you ask for an ad that sounds and/or looks like all other ads, you'll get that. You'll get an ad that takes no risks, won't stand out, won't offend anyone, and one that isn't created according to the direct response wisdom available. And the ad will bomb. Every time.

A professional direct response ad creator is someone who learned a tremendous amount about what works and what doesn't on millions of other people's dimes. We've built a large database of direct response wisdom that can save you a lot of time and money. If you define success as an ad that influences the listener to respond, one that achieves a certain CPO, and support and trust in the creative process, you're much more likely to get successful results. Remember, the question isn't whether you like the ad. It's not even whether the customer likes the ad. The question—the only appropriate criteria for success—is whether the customer buys from you as a result of hearing the ad.

CHAPTER 12

Tips for Getting Started with Your Direct Response Radio Campaign

> Advertising in the final analysis should be news.
> If it is not news it is worthless.
>
> –Adolph S. Ochs, *The International Thesaurus of Quotations*

Do It Yourself vs. Hiring an Agency

The first question to answer is whether to do it yourself or enlist the assistance of an agency. The answer depends on your size and/or your goals for radio advertising. In general, the smaller your business is, the more appropriate the do-it-yourself path is for you. The larger your business, the better off you'll be with the assistance of a direct response radio agency.

Do It Yourself

If your business is smaller, or you're looking for a small contribution to your business from radio advertising, you may be better off with the do-it-yourself approach. This book can be of great assistance to you in navigating that path. You'll need to write and produce your radio ad. You can either find a freelancer to do the writing for you, or you can do it yourself. For production, you should most definitely find a voice talent to create the ad. There are many, many of these people out there, so you'll need to listen to lots of demo reels to select the one with the voice and read that you envision for the spot you wrote. Throughout this process, the Internet is your friend—leverage the search engines to your benefit!

Then you'll need to buy your media. With this book in hand, you now have the right perspective from which to approach it. You may want to pick up a book specifically on radio media buying to assist you further. Select the right formats for your target demographic and identify the stations that fall within them. Since you're smaller, you will be buying airtime in only one market, which will make things more simple. Then it's time to call the stations, gather their listenership information, and start negotiating rates and schedules.

Another resource you may want to consider is Google. At the time of this writing Google is attempting to launch a radio advertising offering that mimics Google's online pay-per-click approach. That means it's an enhanced do-it-yourself way to conduct radio advertising. Whatever you do, follow the instructions in this book, particularly the advice about ensuring your results are trackable so you can learn from your advertising spending.

Hiring a Radio Agency

If your business is of the size and scope that necessitates building a national radio advertising campaign that is generating thousands of leads per week, then you are better off going with a radio advertising agency that specializes in direct response radio.

Why? First, because you will gain access to the agency's significant expertise, which will allow you to begin your campaign much closer to its potential instead of at the very beginning of the learning curve. Second, the agency will be set up to handle the volume and complexity of the media aspects that will be involved in the operation.

Considerations When Hiring an Agency

1. The agency must leverage database technology

This one is very straightforward. If you've read this book, you can understand the need for a robust database infrastructure that enables tracking, analyzing, and reporting of the incredible amount of data produced by a direct response campaign. Do not hire an agency that is using manual entry into Excel spreadsheets to work with the data. You will not receive the information you need to make profit-maximizing decisions.

2. Require a "full data" approach to communicating the data to you

There are two main types of direct response radio advertising agencies. One direct response radio agency business model is called "full data," and the other—a relative newcomer to the scene—is called "black box." They sit on opposite ends of the spectrum in terms of approach and philosophy to direct response radio advertising. These two agency types are different in many ways, but they also have similarities.

As different as these two approaches are, they are the same in one crucial way: they are both successful at procuring the highly discounted media rates that all direct response radio advertisers require for success.

With the black box model, the radio agency commits to buying a certain amount of remnant media (radio airtime) over the course of a year if, in return for that commitment, the station commits to selling the airtime to the agency at a super-low rate. The black box agency is legally on the hook for that amount of media and in effect resells that media to its clients, marking it up by some unknown (and possibly floating) amount. black box agencies won't disclose what they're paying for the media before they mark it up and resell it to clients. In fact, it could be more accurate to call them "brokers" rather than true advertising agencies.

As a result of this business model, clients aren't allowed to see a) what was actually paid for the media in question, b) any detailed station-by-station or spot-by-spot reporting, or c) any specific market, day, or daypart information. With the black box agency, the client is provided only general metrics based on the entire media spend over a particular period. This is where the "black box" name comes from— clients aren't allowed to see any level of detail about what's going on behind the curtain. It's a basic "dollars in, dollars out" set of reporting.

Full data agencies also obtain remnant media rates. However, they approach this process in a different way. Instead of negotiating for the full year and taking on a large and possibly risky obligation to the radio station to purchase a certain amount of media in return for the low rates, the full data agency negotiates on behalf of the each specific client *during the week or two prior to airing*. This labor-intensive "last-minute" approach allows the full data agency to obtain remnant rates, but without the inflexibility or conflicts of interest that a long-term contractual obligation creates. As a result of this approach, the full data agency can provide detailed reporting to clients, showing media performance by a huge array of possible dimensions, such as station, day, daypart, format, geography, call center, ad copy, and so on. This information allows the client to understand what works, when it works, and with whom. This is where the name "full data" comes from.

Full Data Agency	Black Box Agency
Procures remnant rates by "last-minute" media-buying techniques, charges standard agency commission. No hidden, floating margin.	Procures remnant rates via large buying commitments with stations, then marks up and resells to clients.
Provides full data to client so client can reap maximum learning about what's working and what's not, and has mechanism of accountability with agency.	Provides only summary data to clients because of restrictions in the media deals with stations.
Buys media specific to each client using targeted media buys.	Buys media in bulk using untargeted 18+ demographic.
Buys specific media schedules in days and dayparts that history has shown work the best in direct response for that category and station combination.	Buys the leftover media nobody else wanted, regardless of when it falls in the week or hour of the day.
No conflicts of interest. Acts solely in the client's interests.	Conflicts of interest between client and obligation to the station for a certain amount of media.
Week-to-week approach maximizes flexibility, reduces working capital for client.	Month-to-month approach inflexible. Greatly increases the client's working capital requirement.

111

3. Choose substance over flash

It is unfortunate in the agency world that many times pitching a customer is about wining and dining the customer while making big promises. For example, many agencies say they are experts in radio and/or in direct response when they aren't. You will need to do some digging. But one thing is certain. An agency's lavish offices aren't going to get you the best media. Their fast talking and fancy watches aren't going to do it either.

When you choose an agency, choose one based on what matters: deep experience in direct response radio (preferably, that's all it does).

Think of it this way: If the agency is focused on flashiness, it must be hiding something. It's likely to cover up the lack of substance. Don't fall for it.

The last piece of advice we have for you in selecting your agency is "fit." You need to feel comfortable and confident in your agency's ability to build a profitable direct response radio advertising campaign for you. You need to feel like you can talk openly and candidly to your agency representative. After all, if things go as planned, you'll be spending plenty of time interacting with him or her. You should be treated with respect but not in a way that's just to appease you—you want your agency to be honest with you and to tell you if you're off track. The last thing you want is an agency that is out to tell you exactly what you want to hear rather than what the agency's best judgment is.

Your Testing Budget

Perhaps the final piece of information that is pertinent is how much you should expect to spend in the testing phase before you're at a decision point about whether radio is right for your business and/or you're ready to move to the rollout phase.

For creative development, you should budget around $3,500 to develop four initial ads for testing. For media spending, you should be prepared to spend $3,000 to $6,000 per week over a three- to four-week test period for the initial media test. In the aggregate, you should be prepared to commit $20,000 to $24,000 for initial media testing. If the test media delivers revenues at or above your break-even profitability level, then you've gained significant learning at essentially zero cost. If the test media delivers revenues at just 75% of your break-even profitability level, then for less than $8,000 you gained significant learning about how to leverage direct response radio as a profitable venture for your business—gaining invaluable insights about how to build a direct response radio advertising campaign that takes full advantage of the opportunity. This highly favorable risk-reward situation underscores the opportunity direct response radio advertising provides to businesses looking for profitable growth.

BIBLIOGRAPHY

Arbitron, Inc. "Radio Today 2005." www.arbitron.com.

Arbitron, Inc. "Radio Today 2006." www.arbitron.com.

Astor, Brett J., Small, Jeffrey R. "After The Phone Rings," www.strategicmediainc.com, 2007.

Bernbach, William. *Bill Bernbach said.* New York: DDB Needham Worldwide. 1989.

Burnett, Leo. *100 LEO's.* Chicago: McGraw Hill, 1995.

Delaney, Kevin J., McBride, Sarah. "Google, Clear Channel Reach Radio Deal Partnership" *Wall Street Journal*, April 16, 2007, p. B4.

Eicoff, Alvin. *Or Your Money Back.* New York: Crown Publishers, Inc., 1982.

Famina, Jerry Della. *From Those Wonderful Folks Who Gave You Pearl Harbor.* New York: Pocket Books, 1971.

Hammonds, Keith H. "Michael Porter's Big Ideas." *Fast Company*, February 2001.

Lutz, Frank Words That Work New York: Hyperion, 2007.

McGarry, Edmund D., "The Importance of Scientific Method in Advertising," *The Journal of Marketing*, Vol. 1, No. 2, (1936), 82–86.

Media Monitors, LLC. www.mediamonitors.com.

Ogilvy, David. *Ogilvy on Advertising*. New York: Vintage Books. 1985.

Ogilvy, David. *Confessions of an Advertising Man,* New York: Ballantine Books, 1978.

"Scientific method." The American Heritage® Dictionary of the English Language, Fourth Edition. Houghton Mifflin Company, 2004. 28 Sep. 2007.

Tripp, Rhodas Thomas. *The International Thesaurus of Quotations*. New York, NY: Thomas Y. Crowell Company, 1970.

ENDNOTES

[i] See *Wall Street Journal* "Google, Clear Channel Reach Radio Deal Partnership", April 16, 2007.

[ii] Source: Media Monitors LLC., www.mediamonitors.com.

[iii] Arbitron "Radio Today" 2005 and 2006 www.arbitron.com.

[iv] Arbitron "Radio Today" 2005 and 2006 www.arbitron.com.

[v] Fast Company Interview "Michael Porter's Big Ideas" February 2001.

[vi] "scientific method." The American Heritage® Dictionary of the English Language, Fourth Edition. Houghton Mifflin Company, 2004. 28 Sep. 2007.

[vii] McGarry, Edmund D., (1936) "The Importance of Scientific Method in Advertising," *The Journal of Marketing, Vol. 1, No. 2, pp. 82–86.*

[viii]Brett Astor and Jeff Small interview with Scott Badger, principal, KPI Direct www.kpidirect.com, for the article titled "After the Phone Rings".

[ix]Note that no advantage is forever. Today, Dell has "evolved" the direct model to include retail sales.